JESUS IS THERE
THROUGH IT ALL

JESUS IS THERE THROUGH IT ALL

LATASHA HAWKINS

*James (JC) Thomas and Paul Thomas
Book Cover Designer*

Copyright © 2021 by

All rights reserved. No part of this book may be reproduced in any manner whatsoever without written permission except in the case of brief quotations embodied in critical articles and reviews.

First Printing, 2021

I

Jesus Is There, Through It All

Written By: Latasha Arnett Hawkins

This book is dedicated to Jesus Christ who's been there through it all, my family and friends and especially to each of you, for every reader who needs hope or to be reminded of his unfailing love for us.

Table of Contents

Childhood Love
All These Babies
The Race
Marriage Is A Strong Union
Issues, We All Have Them
There Is Always Room To Grow
Selfless to Self-Care
Holiness Is Right
Let Not My Heart Be Troubled
How To Stand With Someone Else
COVID-19, I Was Not Exempt
Lukewarm Just Won't Do
It's A War Going On
To The Reader

Childhood love

Far as I can remember as a child, unconditional love has always been present. At the time I didn't know it was called loved, but I felt it. I grew up in a single parent home, with my mother whom I love dearly, Geraldine Arnett. When I was young attending the latter part of elementary school, my mother, brothers, and I resided with my grandmother Cleo Arnett, another woman I hold so dear to me in my heart and may her soul rest in peace. I remember not knowing that my father was missing from raising me. When God is in the midst of it all, he will not allow you to plant your eyes on things to cause us pain. I didn't realize a father exists until I was old enough to understand what Father's Day meant. By the time I understood the concept of a father, he came to us informing us that he was moving to Florida, not knowing this would be the last time I could recall remember seeing him in my youth.

Outside of my missing father, my mother did not focus on sharing with me what I did not understand. I was here and she was responsible for providing for me. I can recall enjoying my childhood. I remember getting home being asked about doing my homework or studying, not going outside until it was done, and if the sun had already gone down, I could not leave the yard. Life was very exciting as a child because no matter who you saw, if they knew your mother or someone in your family they going to speak and say tell your momma or grandma I said hello. It was safe taking candy from others and riding your bikes up and down the street. Being excited about warm meals and taking bubble baths. You dare not have questioned what chore they told you do, nor did we get allowances. We did not have choices of what we wanted to eat, food was served, and we ate.

Growing up playing with cousins, not caring how you were related. We were so glad to see each other, playing baseball or softball together, hide and seek, tag, hopscotch, jump rope, frisbee, teacher or whatever we wanted to do or be when we grow up. Playing in the neighborhood was safe. Any adult or leader in the neighborhood was respected and you had to obey if they were telling you something that was right. Cousins and friends getting mad at each other, even down to fighting sometimes but the parents didn't take it to heart; they got us together and see what went wrong, made us apologize and figured out where to go from there. If you had a disagreement with your friend, you either stayed friends or don't say nothing at all, but we did not pick at each other and keep it going, that is where that whooping came into to play. You had to listened to your friend parents, rather you talked to them or not.

Love is an action word and people really expressed their concern and feelings for me. I remember my mom was not fortunate to afford a car, but we still got around because of the love from others. One exciting time in my life was going to the fair for the first time. Other kids always talked about it and at the time, we only knew about the small fair going on in the BI-LO parking lot. My best friend, Buffy at the time, was celebrating her birthday and she could choose a friend to take with her to the fair in Statesboro. Out of all people, she chose me. Her mother Mrs. Mary loved her enough, to love me that she asked her older sister Diane to take us. I had the best time of my life; I got on what I thought to be the scariest ride, called 'The Rainbow'. It would take you so far in the air, I thought I saw the entire town of Statesboro. Once you got so high in the air and it would stop, then come back down so fast; felt like it took all my breath away, we were screaming and holding on so tight. I was pressing my feet so hard hoping I did not fall out. Also, this was my first time knowing what a funnel cake was and oh it was so good. The taste of warm sweet bread with powdered sugar on top was delicious. See Statesboro GA was like another state to me because it seemed like that was my very first trip out of Sylvania and I fell asleep on the way back because I was tired of all the fun we had that day.

Love does not look at your circumstances to see rather you should communicate with an individual. I can remember growing up, going places with my grandmother or auntie to Mr. Son Hunter for some bar-b-que and playing with my cousins. While the parents were in the house talking, we knew to stay out of grown folks business; we automatically went out the door and started playing with each other. Love will allow you to embrace each other no matter how long time has passed by from seeing each other. Just knowing were family was enough to keep loving each other and glad of being in each other's company.

Love does not make you wonder why people don't do things with their children. My first Summer vacation was a weekend to remember. I remember having two uncles living in Augusta. My cousin Derrick was going to stay with his dad, Uncle Don, for that weekend and my uncle Waymond and Aunt Pat wanted us to come visit. It was me, my brothers Antwoine and Deondra and my cousin Sharon. My uncle Don came and got us in his Yugo. This car looked so small on the outside, but we all fit in and we all seated comfortably. I remember love made us laugh at each other about small things, but we did not go too far to hurt each other's feeling. My cousin Derrick had this small suitcase that looked like a lunchbox, but he had so many clothes packed. We thought it was so funny but we had a heavy load to take out the trunk of the car once we got to Augusta. We enjoyed ourselves that weekend, even though my cousin Derrick stayed with his dad, we all were together enjoying the weekend.

During your childhood you will experience and discover a lot of things. I remember while staying with my uncle and aunt, it was my first-time hearing and seeing what a water bed look liked. At first, I was scared to sleep on it because I did not want to bust it. I end up meeting a girl that had the same name I did, and she ended up being part of Summer vacation weekend. Love automatically made her feel like she always knew us because if my aunt and uncle thought it was okay for her to stay, so did we.

I love all my family, especially my cousin Christopher Farmer, may his soul rest in peace. His life ended while being an active member in the military. His love for me and my brothers was so heartfelt. He loved my mother so much. He was like the big brother we never had. He always took up time with us and took us to the park and would give us things. Even though he was young, he always uses to tell my mother, that she was a good person and he will always do for us even though she did not asked him. He told me one time that my mother use to keep him, while his mother worked and that is why he was the big brother. We would be so excited seeing his Regal pull up. He spent time with us; rather it was just on the porch in conversation or taking us somewhere.

Going to church was fun for me. My mother didn't go to church much, but she made sure we went. I used to get up on Sunday mornings and watch the gospel quartet show with my grandmother before she would go to church. She always ended up crying, I didn't realize she was worshiping God for his grace and mercy. I would cry along with her and my brothers would get mad at me. My grandma would take us to Waters Grove Baptist Church from time to time. It was hard at times because she was catching a ride and the driver had a full car sometimes. My aunt Josie or Aunt Rosa Bell would make sure we got to church too. I loved going to Saint Andrew Methodist Church located right by the street I use to live on. In the Summertime it is when I use to go because they always had an event called Vacation Bible School, where many kids from all around Screven would come. We would do arts and crafts and learn Bible verses. We would go outside and play and have a good time. Before, going home the treat at the end of the day was the best. It was 'the thrill'; not realizing I could have made the same thing at home, it was small plastic cups filled with frozen Kool-Aid or juice and because the ice had flavor, it was so good. Also, they would have the Feed-A-Kid program where during noontime, you can go get a sack lunch if you were a child, which saved mom from cooking as much.

God loved us so much, that he was there through it all. Hatred and anger was taught. I can never remember my mother saying anything wrong about my absent father. I can never remember worrying where our next meal was coming from. The love of God is for all mankind. He does not have a respected person. Love does not look at what you have, it is felt through the heart and actions. Jesus love for us, was the ultimate sacrifice. His love removed all hurt and scars that might come into our lives. We got to look beyond judging and show love. If we had that childhood love, to forgive as God instructs us; it will allow us to have that same peace I had back then to now. We can't change what others do, but to remember the good, which will allow us to hope for the better. If God was not there, as a child I would have experience being abandoned, but his love is so strong it would deter you from any frustrations. I come to realize that He has been there, through it all. His presence is strong, even when I could not see Him; I could feel His love from my mothers, loved ones and friends' actions.

We as people, have to love others as we want to be loved. The childhood love I received was innocent and genuine. True love will over shadow any bad or wrong in your life. We must continue to carry the unconditional love, just as we did in our childhood.

Parenthood: All These Babies

Parenthood requires a lot of patience and decision making; so I had to learn not to only think of self while raising my children. My life changed so quickly in my youth. Not knowing what to expect or not knowing that a lot of what I thought was going to be good times for me during my high school days would soon take a new direction down another path.

By the age of twenty-four I had already given birth to five blessed children, who have now grown into their own chapters of life. I was a baby having a baby but did not understand the decisions I was making. I acted upon emotions and spare of the moment decisions and never thought about the consequences. I hid my first and second pregnancy, being afraid of what my mother would think and how disappointed she would be of me. Not telling her the truth, even though she asked, made me do other things that were not right. Lying to cover up the truth, will make you think harder than you have too. I could remember the first time, I found out that I was expecting. I did all I could to dodge my mother. I was in high school during my first pregnancy; so, I would be the first one to get up and go to the bus stop. Soon as I would get home, she did not have to ask me twice about chores. I would do what was expected, so I could go to my room to do my homework, pretend I was tired, so I would go to sleep to avoid her. As time began to pass, she noticed me sleeping all the time and began to question me. I always had a response to throw her off. When she cooked, I would go ahead and eat, sometimes not asking for seconds because if I asked for more all the time, I knew her curiosity would grow.

One morning my mother tricked me and told me we were going to go out and eat breakfast before I went to school. She said we were going to be having a mother and daughter moment with my aunt included. We had to leave early because my aunt had to go to work after taking me to school. Out of nowhere, we pulled up to the health department. My smiles went to frowns, we were there before it opened. I can remember, it was on a Thursday morning because that was the day health department did pregnancy test if you fasted. My mother wanted to get me out the house before I ate or drunk anything. She told me, just to tell her the truth, if I thought I was pregnant. I swore up and down that the rumors were a lie and that I was going to prove her wrong and whoever else wrong. We met with the nurse together because my mom told her the concerns she had. The nurse informed my mother of the client confidentiality and asked her to step out. When the results came back and she went over them with me, only thing I can do was sit in silence, knowing I already knew the truth. The nurse asked me, did I want to tell her; instantly, I spoke up and said no. She called my mother back in the office, I put the curtain around me, and she gave her the news. My mom was silent at first, then she started crying. So, the nurse asked her to talk with me because I was afraid and then discussed alternatives. Just know, Jesus has always been there. My mother could have decided to take a life, but she did not. She told the nurse that because I was pregnant, together as a family, we will have to discuss more information at home, and we will figure out something from there. I could see that the decision I made brought hurt to my mom. Being that my mother was a single parent and unemployed at the time, she was already receiving government assistance brought so many emotions in the atmosphere, I could not even look her in the eyes. My aunt was the first person to know, then when we got home my mother called her brother. At first, I was thinking she is really mad, but the more I listen to her and my uncle on the phone, I began to realize she needed someone to comfort her, to listen to her and to encourage her because of the hurt and thoughts of raising another child in the situation we were living in. Tears continued to flow down my eyes as I sat in the living room listening to her on the phone, because my dark secret was out and it brought pain to the one I truly loved, my mother. As, time continued to pass, my mother started teaching me what to expect and that I was not out of the woodwork with her. She still made be accountable as her child. I was still responsible for the chores that she assigned me and still had to raise my child. She made me go to school up until, I woke up one morning in labor. My mother used to give me two hours, when I arrived home from school. She said I had that time frame to complete my homework assignments and my work around the house. She still had to be my mother, while helping me be one.

Having my first daughter and support from the father made it feel to me that we were going to make it. Though we both were young, with family support we would grow to be wiser. My vision of us growing and maturing as young adults' parents became faint the moment, I gave birth to my daughter because her father called me, while I'm in the hospital informing me, he was not ready to become a father. I instantly went ballistic, screaming, pulling, and knocking things down. At that moment, hurt and rage grew in my heart. I could not believe that the person who was there every step of the way during my pregnancy, who made sure I made it to my doctor appointments, came to see me once he got off from work, would walk away from responsibility so easily. I loved my daughter, but anger grew so deep in my heart it caused me to be mad at other males and not trust them. One baby was not enough for me to learn my lesson. Anger made me move on quicker than I thought, but I did not want to give my heart to no one else. When other guys wanted to talk to me, even though I was a mother, it made me feel good and with the attitude to say, 'there is always more fish in the sea'. My anger for one person, did not help me realize what I was doing to myself or the reputation that would soon follow. With that negative attitude, I thought, before any man could ever hurt me, I would enjoy the moment with them and do as I please, not thinking or caring about anyone's feelings but my own. That way of thinking and living has got me five beautiful and blessed children. The sin part did not please God but He was still right there holding me, with his love and forgiveness. He knew I was angry, but my love for my children never wavered.

The immaturity of the fathers and not helping me raising them brought on more pain. While, I was on a rampage having babies after babies, I did not think how my actions may affect how my children will look at relationships when they grow older. Only thing that was running through my mind is I will not get hurt again. Well I did because those one-night stands, turned into me having more children with men uncommitted to me and especially to the children they fathered. I was being selfish for wanting company, to be noticed by men, and having the attitude of 'one man don't stop know show'. I had to come to the realization that I was only hurting me and my children. I was beginning to realize that was not the route I wanted to take.

I remember my mother telling me to stop crying and close my eyes. She said, I want you to start praying to God and know that He is here when no one else will be. She said, close your eyes and imagine, it is just you, your kids and God. In that moment, I started casting my cares upon the Lord. She told me not to even depend on her because I needed to learn to love and raise my children without her. Strength began to kick in, sleepless nights began to disappear. God began to touch the hearts of others, that when my mother was unable to help me, there was always someone else coming to offer a helping hand. God's love for me is way far beyond what I could ever imagine. God has forgiven me for my sins. He even shows me that my love was so strong, he made room for others in my heart. True love did exist with one of my children's father and we end up marrying each other ten years later. He gave me four more stepchildren to help nurture, I helped raise a niece and be an example to my Godchildren.

Raising other children is not easy. When raising a blended family, you must be open-minded and know that your expectations and morals may not mean the same throughout each household. I must be honest; I have dealt with three different mothers of children whom I truly love. With my stepchildren, I had to deal with two other mothers. This task has not always been easy. When you have personal mixed feelings, the children are who suffers the most. We have had many disagreements, wrong on both parts. There have been times when the children was not allowed to come over anymore to the home of where their father resides, because we as adults was not seeing eye to eye. The children were the innocent ones and was being caught in the middle of confusion.

Earlier I wrote, not being married when I had my children, well the other parties were not too so you can imagine all the drama. I thank God for his mercy and grace, giving us time to get right with him. He knew our hearts, wanting what is best for the children but allowing the enemy to have a field day with us, when we supposed to be the leaders to our children. I can speak for me, that I learned through this process of being a stepmother, that I am only responsible for what I teach in my household. I must stand firm on the decisions I make and what happens to them, while being in our care. For example, if that child were misbehaving in our home and received their consequences, I thought it should follow them back home to teach them we as parents was on the same page. When the consequences was not carried out once they got back home, I would get upset or discouraged because I felt that the child was being taught to act different. The conclusion I came up with, when I allowed wisdom to kick in, was to accept that I could not change what was out of my league. I learned to handle what was in front of me and to treat them as I would treat my own kids. While they were in our care that is what I do. I would still make the other mother aware of what is going on, but I did not expect any support on my decisions of how their father and I did things in our home.

With my Godchildren, I never had any trouble with their parents. Raising my niece, was a different thing. We all had an opportunity to pour in her life, but we all had different ways of how we raised our children. Not saying either was right, but somehow with me, mine came with some arguing and misunderstanding. Yet, again we thank God for his presence of making the path right. Also, raising or caring for them during different times in their life, exposed me and my home to things happening all around us and not being aware to things made me to have a better open communication with all the children.

I just give honor to Christ because even in my wrong, his life gave me life and another chance to get it right. When God allowed me to be a mother figure to others, I felt that I was forgiven and that true love for my children, can be shared to others. Not saying their parents do not love them, but he saw enough for me to be part of their life, to instill something in them too. Whether it was for a season or throughout a lifetime, we were able to cross each other's path for a reason. God knew I could show love despite all obstacles that came my way. He knows that my love is genuine and that I mean well, even though I have not always been right. He still saw the best in me. So, to let you know, we mess up in life and do things that are wrong, but you do not have to stay stuck in your sin. Me having all these children out of wedlock and finally repenting for all that fornication, I know that God has forgiven me. He allowed me to love not only mine but others who I truly see as my own; I thank him for this sign, no matter how it came about. My forgiveness allowed me to move forward being the best mother I know how. I love all nine of our children, my Godchildren, and my niece. I will continue to teach them, being there for them to the best of my ability. We just got to be ready to embrace our opportunity to love.

I continue this day giving God the praise because what people thought would turn into a generational curse was not so. I could remember people telling me, that I am going to see how my mother felt by me having these babies staying in her house and that when my children grow up, the same thing was going to happen to me and it was going to be worst. But just know Jesus has and is there through it all. No matter how many times I became pregnant each time I repented and prayed to God to be my guide and provider. When I truly surrendered to Christ, I could remember crying out to him one more time about me having children and being Godly sorry. Reading the scriptures continued to open my eyes to see clearer that when you repent, you try all you can not to keep doing that same sinful act. I was praising him for not giving up on me for continuously repeating the same sin five times, bringing hardship to my family. Even though I know God owes me nothing, I prayed to him to show me a sign, to never allow any of my children to become parents while attending grade school. Each time my children graduated, I felt like that was a sign from the Lord. I would meet my graduating child on field after the graduation ceremony and cry out telling God thank you. I was praising him for answered prayer, one celebrating their accomplishment but mostly knowing and believing that I was truly forgiven. My children understood the yelling and leaping for joy was for the sign God had given me. My fifth child graduated in 2020, neither child has no babies. I know that I did not owe anyone anything or any explanation, but God knew my heart and for that I am grateful.

The Race

The race is not given to the fast or strong, but to those who endures to the end. This scripture has really helped me throughout my life and continues to help put my mind at ease. I have realized in life, that no one was ever set up to fail and what seems to be obstacles and challenges in life are caused by wise and unwise decisions. I had to realize that this race was not about me facing what I see with my eyes, but about the unseen spiritual war going on from the wickedness of the devil. In this race you get tired sometime, but I had to remember to believe the power that work in me. I give God all the praise because when I thought I had to respond, the Holy Spirit says be still and know that I am God. What seem like a long time to others, God is saying I am using some situations to expose and to grow you for other challenges. He will never put no more on us than we can bear. You must learn to be silent and not tongue wrestle with others about what they think when you know the truth.

You ever noticed during sports event; everybody starts off at the same starting point. Every sport scores starts off with zero and even at the end of the time frame that is given, each has an ending result. There is always one winner during the competitions. No matter the sport one team is going to be first and one team is going to be ranked last, but the beauty of it, they never stop playing their position because of their rank. For instance, during track each runner position themselves to take off, they look ahead to see where the finish line and began to think of a strategy of how they're going to beat their opponent. One may decide to go slow around the curve and then take off fast on the straight way, and then you may have another who decides to go fast the entire time. One thing for sure they all have in common is finishing. During the race, the runners are sprinting to the finish line, only one becomes first and breaks the rope, but the others continue to run to the finish line regardless of what place they arrive. No matter rather they win or lose, it still does not stop them from competing in the next race. Their mind is already set that there will be a better opportunity next time and they began working on how they could be the next winner. They do not stay stuck in that moment; they look forward to the next race. They continue to practice and keep moving forward to what is next on the schedule.

In my life, I have started over so many times when it came to raising my children. By each having different personalities, I had to stop and think how I am going to approach them when it came to teaching them life lessons, disciplining them, or just conversing with them. Anytime I had to evaluate my future career, I had to consider some things before making the wrong move. No matter what decisions in life, you must start from somewhere. Your ending will be your result, depending upon the moves you make. Every result may not end like you expected, but you can be sure to rejoice for not giving up. I had to learn in life, that people have different ideas and different goals for their future. It is not who succeed first, just allow God to embrace your timing and let him bless you when it is your time. Making different decisions can speed or slow your expectations in life. As for me, being a teenage mom, I had to take different routes in finding a job to help me raise my children. I did not graduate from high school; I saw the need of becoming employed to help raise two children by the age of sixteen. While running this life as a young mother, I was not only running alone, I had children that were running with me, and so I had to be patient with them. I had to slow down and not leave them behind. Because they are here, my mindset had to change; they now had to be part of my decision making. I started working at McDonald's to help make ends meet in my mother household. I had enough common sense, not to think I was grown enough, not to listen and learn from others who were already parents. Their concern and wisdom helped me along the way. On this race, I could have easily quit and gave up my children, but because God allowed me to have them, He had to see fit that I was going to be able to take care of them by showing love, nurture, teaching them and providing for them. He knows that in this race, I am going to continue staying at a pace to allow him to show me spiritually when to teach, rebuke and be there for them. God gave me enough sense that I could not expect to get this job that required certain skills and degrees if I had quit school. I had enough wisdom to know, I still had to work, and employment at McDonald's was one curve that I was passing to help me make it on to the next stretch. I ran along this path, until I found another direction that was right to go on.

I truly thank my mom, Geraldine Arnett for being my number one supporter, even when I was disappointing her. She was doing all she could to be my mother, while helping me become a great mother. She did not have to accept my wrongdoing in falling in the teenage pregnancy population, but her love for me reached beyond my faults. My children did not ask to be here, and it was my responsibility to make them part of my life and to teach them all I know to do right. While running this race, I continue to make some wrong decisions and kept stepping over in someone else lane and always find myself falling towards mine and getting back up from where I left off. During this race, I continue to not stay in my own lane, I began to follow others or become part of the norm, whatever the crowd was doing. That is how I find myself being a young mother of five children by the age of twenty-four. During my journey, while I am still running this race, I had to do what was necessary to get me a better job. I was not able to walk with my high school graduating class nor receive my high school diploma, but I went to Ogeechee Technical Institute Adult Literacy program to earn my GED, is equivalent to a high school diploma. Once I received my GED, I later decided to attend college to obtain an associate's degree. While deciding to go to college, I knew I still had to work to financially provide for my children and me so I maintained my employment at McDonald's. It was time for me to carry the torch of being accountable as a mother, provider, still love myself in meeting my goals in life and being an example to the little ones'. I had to teach them not to fall over the same hurdles I did and to redirect them back to positive living.

God has created each of us with a purpose. We all have an assignment to be completed and our starting point in life is spiritually developing a relationship with him, through accepting salvation and learning how to live Holy. The race for us is staying in our own lane and going the speed that God expects us to go. We all have a starting point and what we do while running this race will determine when to go fast, slow, and how to pace yourself in every decision you make. Running life properly and spiritually with guidance, you don't have to worry about coming around nobody. God wants us to just be part of the race, trusting him to guide our every footstep. He wants us to make every second count in our lives. You don't have to be first in this race to win, you just got to learn to endure and never stop running.

This race in life is not always going to be easy because you are not always the one running it alone. There is going to be some bumps in the road, or some ditches to cause you to fall but what you do and who you depend on makes the difference. God is the only one who knows the plans for you. This race has to be totally dependent upon Christ to intercede to the Father, which is in heaven, to direct your path. God did not want me to look to the left or the right to see who was ahead of me, behind me, or beside me, He wanted me to keep running this course depending on him. It does not matter who's on the sideline cheering you on or shouting your name to distract you with negative thoughts trying to make you lose focus; He wants you to look straight ahead to Him. He tells us in His Word, the way to him is straight and narrow, but to hell is wide and broad. We cannot get caught up on how everyone is doing, we should be focusing on our life journey. It is ok to cheer others on because we should all be building each other up to do good along this race. During this race, God will send people to cheer you on, to motivate you to do better; but just remember He is always available to listen, to seek for direction, and to push you to move forward. Keep on running if I can you can.

Marriage Is a Strong Union

You got to have true love in your heart and a prayer life to withstand the test and trials against the plots of the enemy. When getting married, I truly loved my husband but did not know how to fight for my marriage. On the outside, I resembled attributes what one would consider to be "wifey material", because I was a person with good deeds, but come to realize without God nothing is possible. My husband and I have had many disagreements and misunderstanding of each other in our marriage, which caused us to make unwise choices that could have ultimately damage our covenant before God. But In a marriage, you got to learn who holds it together. In Ecclesiastes 4:12, the scripture lets us know that God is that string to wrap around us. We did not fully understand, what that meant towards our marriage. We looked at marriage as if we were happy and we understood each other, everything would be fine. We agreed that when we disagreed on something, we will face it later, but during the test and trails, how quickly we forgot the vows we made before God, just because we were not in a happy moment. We learned in our marriage, that we were fighting the wrong way. Instead of honoring our vows and covenant, we were trying to prove who was right, who get the last word, or watch I show you kind of attitude during emotional and heated moments. We had lost focus, allowing the devil in to try and destroy what God had ordain and blessed from the beginning of time.

There were times we did not want to stick it out and began plotting against each other. Trying to put on the best face in front of the children and doing things sneaky behind each other's back, we allowed our negative feelings to grow towards one another. We knew God was not in the mist of our marriage because He do not bless in any mess. No matter how much we tried to make excuses of why we did what we did, God honors marriage. We came to realize, a lot of our struggles and downfall came because of our personal disobedience toward the marriage. Just because one did wrong, do not mean the other had too. We allowed anger and outside influences tell us to give it up. In our marriage when we first got married being in our twenties, young still trying to learn and mature in our own lives we knew we was not ready but did it anyway. We were not ready to let our family and friends go, to be fully committed in building our own family letting God lead. We let some issues destroy time we cannot take back. We let unmarried people, who never experience sacred vows, talk us into doing things in our vulnerable state of mind. In our marriage, we were going back and forth, cheating on each other; calling other friends and family when we get mad at each other, talking about each other. It is amazing to find out what outsiders truly thought of our marriage. Because during those not so good moments, you will have some ready to cloak for you. It would be some helping you hide from the other spouse while they look you right in the face like they have not seen them. We still could not blame no one or anything but ourselves for the struggles we allowed to happen.

I thank God through his son Jesus interceding on our behalf, in our toughest time He has always been there interceding for us. When we began to come together and say what we really want and how we truly feel for each other, the words renewed our vows and faith kicked in. Through life challenges, you got to learn to seek counsel from the Lord. He said go to the elders for a report. You got to seek counsel through prayer and talk to other married people who have overcome through trusting God to fight your battles. My husband and I, separated before, but the love from within will never let us call it quits. We realized that it was the spiritual forces of the enemy in dark places that made us blind. When we began to bend on our knees together and speak life to each other, it then led us to fight against the issues in our marriage and not against one another. We are not perfect, but we are wiser. We have come to realize that through it all, the presence of God has always been there and it was us who chose to ignore his counsel through the word on how to fight against the wiles of the devil. We learned that the little foxes are what destroys the vine. We allowed a little misconception on our own opinions or thoughts to explode into something bigger than it ever should have been.

As, I write these words of encouragement to you, we still have celebrated 15 years and counting. The best of our story is still not told of the love that God has between a husband and a wife. So, I want to share with you seven life lessons that I have grown to learn, through the test and trials. My husband and I went live on social media talking about fourteen things we learned by discussing seven practical points each, that we have grown to know overtime through our marriage. As I discuss, seven of those points; I pray that it be a blessing to you and that you look deeper within yourself. In order to be part of someone else, you first must learn self.

First thing, I learn through the years is that I could not ask God to restore our marriage and then I am still trying to handle things on my own. Either I am going to allow God to fix what is broken or either go by what I see and do what I think is best. It will never work because then I will be doing things on my own and not coming together as one. One of the biggest mistakes we made is pretending everything was alright. We were so busy trying to show the children and our family, what it looked like to be a good marriage; til we ignored the fact that the we were letting the enemy get the best of our relationship. We got lost in our own cover-up until we thought it was okay

Our trials lasted so long, what could have been a season of hurt and pain has been stretched way beyond what we could imagined. But, thank you Jesus for interceding as God to forgive us for when we don't know what to do. Addiction to drugs and trust played a big part to our marriage being broken and we swept it under the rug instead of sweeping the corruption and the side of effects up and giving it back to the devil, and resisting his tactics showing him that he can't dwell there no more. We allowed him to make us believe; as long as we put the best on the outside it was okay, that it was no one else business anyway and all along they already out there seeing what we don't know about each other. If you're going to let God restore, we have to forsake all. Give all the bad and ugliness of the marriage.

Number two: let my husband lead. I learn it is a difference in letting him be the head and allowing him to control. God wanted me to trust him, when he gave man the authority to lead his household to Christ. When we got married, we were sinners. I gave my life to Christ and accepted salvation. It was hard for me to leave the dark side of this world, and even harder because my husband decided to stay in the world. I felt we were not equally bonded anymore and did not know how to handle it. I was a renewed woman learning the gospel of Christ, trying to get a better understanding of the purpose in my life. Then on the other hand I would have to come home to my husband playing music I no longer listen or him going places I no longer wanted to visit. I had to learn to not be the one not to cast the first stone and to not look down on the decisions he was making. I had to learn that if it was not against God's word or bringing harm to me or our family, that his thoughts and decisions were just as important as mine. I know that he loved his children and I and would not want anything to happen. He was a provider and nurturer just like I was. As a woman, having children at a young age, I become independent faster and had to double check my surroundings because of my kids. I had a habit, every time my husband would go pay a bill or decide on chores for the family or plan on doing something with family, I always try to ask questions or explain in my own words what he meant. Our children used to tell me, mom we understand daddy; we don't always need a second conversation to validate. If they did not understand something, they would gladly let me know.

Number three, being faithful to each other; not letting temptation that come our way make us do wrong. There has been times that my husband and I was not around each other that taught me how God who is always watching and that I got to give an account for what I do. It allowed me to know that, through separation or just being apart that there is morals that I believe in and being faithful is one of them. Now it has not always been easy to do but the more you trust God the more you will become faithful to your marriage. Not letting one moment of fun and pleasure destroy what would be victory of our marriage.

Number four: Being an active listener to each other. Communication is a key to the marriage. I know how important it is to listen to each other person, and how it will allow you to self-evaluate to better understand who you are and what the other spouse is saying. Listening to what the other person has to say, doesn't mean that you are wrong, but it lets you know their opinion and thoughts matter too. When being an active listener, it helps listen to comprehend or understand instead of listening to respond. Every conversation does not need a response. If you are actively listening to your spouse, your action will reflect on your understanding of what the other is saying.

Number five: Praying for one another. It is clear that living holy is an individual decision and praying to God is a communication between you and Him. In a marriage because we are no longer two but one, we must take time out to pray for each other. My husband and I have decided not to let a day go by without praying over each other. When he pray, he is talking with God about me and when I pray, I am talking to God about him. Prayer is what makes this marriage a stronger union because we allows everyone to face the truth, and if a problem exist it's time to start coming against it by doing the right thing and getting help if need to.

know that we are talking directly to the one who can protect us keep our marriage together. We know in prayer we connect to one who sees and knows all things. Prayer has not always been e because those circumstances such as addiction and trust took u far into shame and being lost of not knowing how to call on h It allowed our marriage to be broken and it lead to other pain our family. Our children seeing what division looks like, not kno ing how to fight and respond the right way to disagreements, la of communication and having trust issues among others. What thought we had under control on our own and being in denial abo it led to poor and outcome decisions. Prayer is changing that b cause we now know how to pray and how to respond. Even thou others may remember when, but as long as our Father has forgive us and we telling him all about it; we could vision our future an walk in it with joy, knowing trouble and the devil scheme didn't las

Number six: Forever learning each other. We know that we can turn back the hands of time, yesterday is gone. We know that w cannot make up for lost time, but what we do know that every day i a new day. If you are reading this, today is a new day to live and ge it right with each other by consulting the Father which is in Heaven The more we honor God, the more we will honor our marriage. We know the more we learn of God, the more we will change within ourselves and the more the marriage will change because we learn new things about each other. If God is with us, who can be against us and who shall we be afraid of. Our present help is giving all our concerns to Jesus who always intercedes for us asking God to give us another opportunity with each other.

Number seven: Honesty and admitting our faults. God watches everything, so why not being honest with each other, so you can fight for your marriage and the issue. We cannot hide anything from God, so bring awareness and truth to each other helps us to be open and committed to each other. When being honest with each other it

Issues, We All Have Them

Different stories in the Bible really helps me during my difficult times of facing issues in my life. I like this story particularly with the woman with the issue of blood because we as people have been judged and cut off from others because of what they have heard or thought they knew. The issues in my life could have been considered unclean to others, which could've caused them to form thoughts and opinion to not deal with me. Not knowing the truth, but just because a certain amount of people was thinking it or believe it, that something got to be true. I have faced difficult issues in my life because of unwise decisions I've made that did not line up with God's purpose for my life. In my life, difficult times has faced my family and I. We must remember, the devil tramples the earth to kill, steal and destroy. Every issue in life does not mean it is a punishment. Sometimes we as people are being used as a living testimony. Our God sees our needs to help in developing our full potential and purpose.

Some circumstances in life last longer than others. But how you respond to it makes the difference. While I was reading the story about the lady with the issue of blood in the Bible; it began to make me realize that I was stronger than I may thought, even though tough times may come. Every time she went to another physician, it led me to believe that she would get her answer. But the downside to me was, not that the doctors knew how to help with her issues, but she would give all she had for help. How many issues have we dealt with, that we felt the need to go to others; they listen and then at the end, still not able to help you? Sometimes people want to hear your issues with no intentions of helping and others really want to help but they just can't. Imagine being cut off from your love ones or being separated from others. No support, no uplifting, no one really understanding that it doesn't changed the good of you because of the issues. I could relate to the woman in the parable. People hearing bits of your issues, not talking with you but talking against you, or agreeing with others that too do not know what is going on. Jesus is the ultimate sacrifice who have paved the way for you and me. The hope that we need to go on is being in his presence, knowing that he is available to us.

This story helped me to realize, you can't tell people your issues. You got to know who to go to for encouragement, by being guided by the Holy Spirit of whom to talk and pray with you on your issues. Faith comes by believing and we as people got to trust in our higher power, the one who sits high and watches all, God. Any issue in life could be dealt with; we have to recognize that he has always been here and to trust the outcome because he knows all.

All my issues have not been solved but I will keep casting my cares upon him and not given up. One issue, I struggle with in life is my health and wellness. I've been facing this issue for a very long time, even longer than the woman with the issue of blood. I got to pray and fight this battle daily, not when I want too. By seeking Christ's directions, making faith moves such as changing my eating habit, exercising, and having a peace of mind, I believe it can be done. For me to lose this weight, I got to do something. I know he can help me lose this weight, and through my actions and the strength He gives me, I will. I will not be bound by obesity but will walk away from my issue of struggling with weight. Through faith, I will be able to walk a longer distance, and hopefully someday participate in a marathon. I speak to this issue and tell it to leave me alone, I trust Christ to intercede on my behalf and know through prayer and trusting him, I can do whatever I put my mind too.

I have learned that one issue could bring on another issue. That is why it is very important to not hide the fact when problems are taking place in our lives. As I battle with being healthier, doubt once crept into my mind because I continued to mess up diet after diet.

Instead of looking at my life as changing, doubt began to ponder in the mind and then I began to look at what I see in the mirror instead of trying. Doubt, will cause you to give up on yourself before getting started. I have to encourage myself daily. I have to change my way of thinking. I was so caught up on the numbers on the scale, instead of taking my journey one day at time. I wanted that quick weight drop and soon as three to four weeks pass by, I'm back on an eating spree. I have learned not to doubt my progress and kick diets to the curve and to just exercise as much as I can, drink more water, and eat in moderation.

Doubt led to another issue of having anxiety attacks. By not being pleased at what I saw in the mirror, I began to tell myself I was looking bigger than I appeared to be. This made me get upset at times, especially when it was time to try on clothes in the store. Suddenly, I will be home and began thinking so hard on my experience for that day, then I would start feeling heavier than I was and out of nowhere I am crying. I would start breathing fast, trying to calm myself down by the fear if I go to sleep something would happen to me. But I thank Jesus for my support system, that anxiety has truly left me.

Jesus is truly there when you need him. Either we're going to trust him or give up. Jesus allowed my family to encourage me, by supporting me. Sometimes, we will all exercise as a family and then other times, each of them will take different days to walk with me. I am so glad to get the phone call from my love ones, asking about the different ways I'm moving forward against the issue of unhealthiness. Some of the ideas given, I've used, and it has pushed me to do better and to do more.

You may be dealing with an issue right now in your life that you think, it just no way out or no help in this situation. I encourage you not to give up or give in to the issue, but to be aware of it and think of what positive things you can do to do away with any negative thoughts about it. It may not change right then, but if you keep a positive outlook and knowing Jesus is right there something will change. You just got to believe.

There is always room to grow

I used to say,' life is what you make it'; that statement has become more positive than negative the older I get. I heard this statement growing up and thought it to be wise, but what I am learning now, is based on your purpose in life, what you make of it could be a blessing or a curse.

As I spiritually grow, I have learned over the years to accept the life God has for me There is life after this natural death and I want to have eternal gain, which will be to rejoice every day, worshiping my creator, crying holy and being in the presence of my King. I can choose to have a positive life on this earth, being a well abiding citizen, doing good for myself and to others around me, but will that allow me to get to my final destination, Heaven? No. I have read somewhere in the Holy Bible that doing good deeds in front of others are not going to get you there. You can be a kind, helpful, loving person in which you have never gotten in trouble, or gotten a ticket, not even siting at silent lunch growing up, always giving towards charities with so many hours of volunteer community service, but if you have not totally surrendered to Christ, accepting salvation and living holy acceptable to Christ, your citizenship has stopped on earth. That is just like the rich man in the Bible, who abide by the laws and was a good man and he had the conversation with Jesus, asking him how can he enter into the kingdom of Heaven? When Jesus told him to give up all he had, he was not ready to surrender all. I'm not saying stop being good or being a positive influence to others, I am just saying there is always room to grow spiritually.

I can truly say, I am not where I used to be, but there is always room to grow. I want to be able to share with you, not to give up because you have not made it where you think you belong or should have accomplished; as long as you are breathing you still have time to get it right. Back to my statement, life is what you make it depends on who you are trusting. Are you totaling depending on self to make it in life or are you trusting in a higher power who knows all. As I testify to you about three things that I have outgrown, there are so many ways that I know that through it all he has always been there. Even when I did not recognize him or gave him honor or been obedience to his direction, his mercy and grace kept me.

One, growing up in my youth I was a teenager when I began having children and all my children out of wedlock. I did not get married until after the birth of all my children. But through it all, Christ has always been there interceding for me to be a good parent and giving me instructions on how to raise my children in a way they should conduct themselves. He knew, I had a chance in my future. He interceded to the father in Heaven on my behalf to continue forgiving me for my sins, even when I did not deserve a second chance because of my careless, unwise decision being involved with many different partners in my life during different time frames in my life. I gave a piece of me to others for a moment, not worrying about the outcome or what could happen. God knew my future, that is why I could be a witness, that He has always been there. I'm not boasting about my wrong, because it is a sin to be intimate and not be married, it's called fornication. I kept repeating the choices over and over, getting the same results. When, I began to develop a relationship with Christ, the more I became aware of my sins. With common sense, I knew it was wrong and not setting good example for my children; but realistically and spiritually I did not understand the deepness of my sins. But through it all I give God the glory. He still allowed me to become a better person. The more I became a better parent and being accountable, plus taking full responsibility in raising my children, the more I wanted to do right than wrong. I learned during this time, I could be causing trouble for my children by not being in a relationship with their fathers, they might have other siblings out there not ever being able to meet; having people older than them not liking them for no reason because they did not ask to be here; not only would it be hurting my children, my wrong could cause hurt in other families. It's important to be connected to the true source of help, allowing the Word of God and living in a way to please God to be a better you. I want in life is to receive my blessing from God, giving me the strong will to teach my children they don't have to go out and have five children with four different daddies. See God did not count me out through my bad, he told me there was an escape way since the beginning. I learned that through his word.

Hatred was another part of my life that I had to grow from, and I thank God for being here showering his love toward me when I was focusing on other distractions in my life. Being hurt or being betrayed by one's action or regretful decisions I made in my life caused me to go from being angry to having a hatred heart. It definitely will stop you from experiencing the presence of God and having a peaceful life. While reading the Bible, I began to understand that sometimes things happen to you, that is beyond your control. Your reaction will determine how mature and wise you are of how to respond to the situation. I have had people look at me, use me, and lie to my face repeatedly. My love toward them never wavered, but my trust in them continue to be crushed, which caused me to feel some type of way until it turned from not wanting to be around them to hating them. Hurt and to be hurt will cause you to lose focus and change your life in a direction which you should not take.

Even times in my life, when I kept making the same mistakes over and over, it caused me to not even like myself because of being disappointed. Hatred is a bitter and unpleasant feeling that clouds your heart, that blocks you from hearing the voice of God and fully understanding who you are. I am so glad, that He has always been there. I could have made wrong decisions out of life, where I could have been in unknown places that I didn't deserve but because of Jesus interceding on my behalf, I was covered because of his mercy and love. It was not my doing of escaping from hardship or on my way to hell, it was Him standing in the gap for me because he knew that I was lost, he knew that it was my emotions and what I seen happening to me and around me through the natural eyes that left this cold feeling within in me. God be the glory for his love. He did not like this sin in me, he doesn't dwell in the presence of sin. His love and the purpose is what kept me from not being cut off and losing my life before getting it right. The more I developed a relationship with God, I realize that the only person I was hurting was myself. I came to realized that I am accountable for what I do in life, not others even if wrongdoing was done to me. Hatred is something you can't see at first, it develops from within and starts to affect your decision making and judgement toward others. It can drain you and hinder you from living freely from negative thoughts, which can lead to stress, health problems, ongoing anger, and disappointment. I realized that repenting for this horrible sin of hatred and forgiving myself and others was the only way I will be set free. This is not just saying it, but you must discipline and remind yourself that you're not in control or have the last say. Through his patience with me, giving me a chance to be redeemed from such thing as hatred has allowed me to love all mankind. Now I know that even in my brokenness, my prayers and cries should have been confined to Jesus. I'm not saying that you can't have a conversation with individuals whom caused pain or hurt to you; sometimes that make it better, it's a win situation. You are helping others to know what they need help and saving others from developing hatred in their heart. God is concerned with how we react. He wants us all to love each other. This day, start talking to Christ in prayer telling him about your feelings and choices you plan to make towards someone or self; trust me the inner being, the Holy Spirit, is going to let you know. We must have an open mind and heart to understand his timing and direction. Because I love the Lord and He loves me, I can tell you that I have grown and will keep trusting in him to see me through.

Lastly making it clear, I know that I am not God, but learning how to be led by him is a progress that I learn daily. I know that we are not on this earth to be mean or selfish. We are here to encourage, building others up, leading them to Christ and letting him direct their every being. I found myself, learning not knowing how to say no to others, letting my emotions get in the way by feeling sympathetic about their situation, trying to do all I can to help them. I learned that anything you do in life, you must consult with the father and our way to him is through his son Jesus for direction in making the best decision. He send you answers from reading the Bible, through prayer, listening to his voice, through sermons at church, having conversation with others, listening to other people life testimonies and so many other ways. We do not always get an answer right away. I found myself doing things that I thought was right, by helping others financially and through the natural. Sometimes God want us to direct them to him, through our testimonies, praying with them which is leading to a spiritual dependence upon him not us. Redirecting others back to where our help come from. I am still growing in this area because I do not want to get in the way of God, looking at that person situation and feel if they could see the help, everything is going to be okay. I learned by helping everyone every time they confine in me, was draining me by trying to solve their problems. I'm running around doing all the foot work, when God wanted to use me to show them some guidance. I truly believe God has put people in my path to help, but how I help them is where I let my feelings get in the way. I have learned to be empathic with people and not sympathetic with them. All this came by growing. Mankind can go but so far in being there for someone, everything should lead back to giving God glory, knowing He is all knowing.

In the beginning, I wrote 'there is always room to grow and that life is what you make of it'. Living your best life, is beyond meeting your goals, having lavish materialistic things. I'm not putting down anyone from which they work hard for to get what they want. I know we should have life more abundantly. My encouragement is that you have all your heart desires and more. If we learn how to trust and live for the one who has the final say of our destination to guide us in spirit and truth. Just remember He is always there, when no one else is, and as we look to him, our better days will come. If all you want in life is to accomplish all your earthly goals, then continue to do your best, but if you are wondering where you end up after physical death, then your best life is what you allow God to make of it, this is why there's always room to grow.

Selfless to Self-Care

I am now learning how to make time for self. Life will be more productive for me and will help limit the negativity that I am exposed too. I am now learning that I have been very bitter to myself, lost out on a lot of opportunities, and have allowed blessings that God intended for me to pass me by. I know that I am not forgotten and know that there is a purpose just for me. I have experience and been through so much for me to just accept or just go by what we call the norm. I was predestined before I entered my mother's womb. I was created by the best and know that I am authentic and original, there is no other like me. I am not going to just sit on the gift that God has given me or to allow the view of others stop me because of what they heard, seen or believe about me. I know my life is not my own, and I know that God is expecting my light to shine. I know I'm forgiven for all my sins. God doesn't remember them far as the west from the east. I am headed in the path of righteousness. As, I continue to seek for the Father's will to be done in my life, I know that I must keep moving forward.

Situations have happened in my life that caused me to lose focus on me. I am somebody just like everyone else. I am in a position now, to not look at what I have or what I want; but to a life by doing right by God, while having a peace of mind and walking upright that is pleasing to him. I have neglected myself in the natural and spiritual, and this season I am going to get everything that belongs to me. I am no longer allowing doubt and fear to cloud my trust and thoughts in not fulfilling the Father plans for me and enjoying life to the fullest on this earth and in Heaven.

Some sacrifices are worth it. Being a mother, I am obligated and accountable for raising my children and teaching them how to do things and make decisions. The older my children get or talking with my husband, they tell me all the time, 'you don't really do anything for yourself.' They would plan things for me, sometimes I would follow through and sometimes I didn't. Even though some are teenagers and majority of my children is grown, I still don't do much. Every day is not promise, so I am learning to do whatever I can in that day in which I live. Neither one knows our last day on earth, so I am learning to make my day count.

The bible says in Proverbs 3:15 'She is more precious than rubies; and all the things thou canst desire are not to be compared unto her.' In researching rubies, I come to realize their value. They are in very high demand, just as much as diamonds. Rubies gemstone is unique and has a beautiful strong red color. Rubies were known for love, energy amongst other things. The word of God tells us that we as women are more than, meaning we are way better than anything on this earth that can be brought with a prize. We are priceless, we cannot be valued or compared to anything. As a woman, I've come to realize that I am important and that through my actions and voice, I too can empower others as well as allowing others to empower me. I believe that everything I been through will be able to help the next person. It doesn't matter if you are a male or female, you have an assignment to complete and the confidence to walk in it. I can do nothing on my own, but through Christ Jesus it is doable. I truly believe there is room for everyone to do good, to set an example, and have a positive attitude and outcome to anything they put their mind too. Life has a way of making you realize that it is not too late to do what your heart seeks. I still got time to cast my cares to the Lord concerning my heart desires. Others and I could have some similarities or things in common, but we still are two different individuals. I know that God wants and will continue using me. I am in demand, as a woman of God he wants the words I say be acceptable to him. Women have a place in the Earth, and I tend to make my mark.

I will do all I can to take care of me, from being connected to my true source, through improving my health and well-being, being joyful and not allowing anything or anyone to tamper with my happiness. I am learning to let go and let God fight my battles. Sometimes all I need is some quietness, to catch some fresh air. No matter what is for me, it is for me and I plan to take time for self. I thank God for always being here, upholding me and lifting me up during the times I forgot to. His presence has always made me strong. It has been times where I felt exhausted physically and spiritually and did not know how I was going to make it, but because of his love and him being my present help, he strengthen me from within and spoke to my heart to keep pressing on. Through his words of encouragement and direction, I know that I could not fail. It is very important to each of us to know our limits. One day, I woke up and realize that if I have lost focus on me, in doing so much of helping others that it has cause others to trust in me of making a way, instead of the true help. People have different consequences according to the decisions they make in life and if I am doing all I can to help them, sometimes that cause them to deter from what God is really trying to teach them or show them.

There are some things in life that I want to accomplish, which is going to cause dedication, research, and time. Making time for myself, would lead me to think more clearer of which path and choices I need to make in completing my goals and purpose. I encourage you to know that God is here and hears your prayers and heart. We got to learn how to seek the Father before making decisions. Sometimes you do not get an answer right then; this teaches me patience and let me know that I need to slow down. If I never taking the time for myself, I would not be able to have written these encouraging words to you, to hold on and know your limit. To let you know that you deserve to be heard and taken care of too. Take the time to self-examine your lifestyle, the decision you make to see if you made time for yourself or just making quick decisions. You are important and never forget that.

Holiness Is Right

One might say, what is holiness? Holiness to me is living a clean and truthful life. With all the things happening in this world, I want to walk a path that is narrow and a way to look straight forward. Living a holy life requires you to not think on your own but to put your trust in Jesus. It teaches you to expect greater than what you see. In order for me to be holy, I have learned that I first had to surrender. Surrender what, you might ask; that I no longer live by my ways but to spiritually be led by the Holy Spirit. I had to repent for all the wrong things, I've done in life. I had to be truly sorrowful for everything that did not please God. I had to confess my sins, letting the Father know what I have done wrong. In order for me to change, I first had to acknowledge that I no longer want to keep doing those sinful things anymore. Am, I perfect? No. I still must repent daily because sometimes I may do something that does not agree with God expectations of me, without being aware of my sins. This way, I know that through continuing reading his word, praying to him, and allowing the spirit to guide me to the truth; I will learn of my errors.

Another way for me to learn to live holy was to accept the Father which is in Heaven, son Jesus Christ as my personal Savior, and to believe that he came from Heaven to die on the cross for my sins. I believe He died one day and rose on the third day with all power in his hands, ascended to heaven to sit at the right sight of God, and that he still lives today. I never argue with what another person belief or faith. I am so caught up in living that I don't have time debating with anyone on how they choose to live. I try to let the light of God shine in me, so when others ask how I made it this far the opportunity to introduce them to my Savior will be present. This would give me a chance to let them know the same opportunity awaits.

Also, I have to believe that the Holy Bible is God inspired word to teach and show me how to make effective decisions in this life. The Bible teaches me all that I need to know. I have not read the entire Holy Bible yet, but I am doing all I can to get right from which I have learned thus far. I don't want to read the book, take a quiz to show everybody I know the Holy Bible from Genesis to Revelation and not apply His word to my daily living. I am aware that things just do not all of a sudden happen in our lives. Some days could be peaceful, then sometimes you wake up feeling like life is upside down and you did not ask for those chaotic issues to occur in your life. That is why, I can't just trust my ways but to believe in someone who is in a higher place than me, to look down and see what's going on and give me the strength to endure and to protect me.

Holiness to me, is doing all I can not to cause harm to anyone. To abide by God's word. The Holy Bible is not hard to understand, you got to take the time to read it and apply the wisdom that he gives us to our daily living. You cannot just pick certain scriptures out of the Bible, that you know you can be strong in and live that part. You got to understand it as a whole. Somewhere, I read in the scripture, that God is not an author of confusion. So, I don't try to argue with other people from other books, from which they read and abide by. I truly believe, loving others has nothing to do what they study. Everyone has to answer for themselves, but I was taught to forgive, love and keep moving forward. The more you began to seek the truth, the more things you would stop doing to have an afterlife. In Matthew 18:3, scriptures say 'Unless, you turn from your sins and become like little children, you will never get into the Kingdom of Heaven.' It is not talking about being physically born again, but to accept that you have decided to surrender doing things your way. God's way will require you to have an open mind, and just like little children and babies not able to fend on their own, you too must understand that through, God's holy word he'll direct you in the way you should go.

You're not expected to know everything overnight, but to take the time to develop a relationship with Jesus.

Holiness requires you to set yourself apart from doing evil acts, learning to pray for self-discipline, and not so easily getting caught up in things that is not of God. I came to realize that everyone on this earth, I want to live holy. I must remember because I've grown in certain areas, it is not too late for others to grow too. When you began to shift your thoughts in wanting to do things right; you will learn not to respond by emotions. I must remember that I have not always been as strong as I am now. During, my lifetime, I have done the same thing to others that have been done to me. Was it right, no but one day, I chose to live a more peaceful life. I want to live in such a way to make my soul rejoice, not to only be happy, but to have my mind, heart, and soul line up on one accord. Holiness required me not to tolerate sin or take part in it. It is important to pray daily and do not take part in anything ungodly. I know right and wrong is upon this earth but living a Holy life will help you stay connected to God. Holiness will make you want to obey God's word. Holiness will keep you from doing the same wrong repeatedly. People sin in many ways, wrong is wrong. Some think because they never got caught or no one see's them, it is okay. Holiness would make you want to stop those dark secrets, from doing drugs, committing adultery or fornication, picking at other people by the way they look or what they wear, talking about people in front of them or bashing them behind their backs. Living Holy will turn you away from any sin, keep reading the Holy Bible, it will tell you what is not of God. It is very important to know that holiness will keep you from causing harm to self and others. I hope that you will examine yourself and ask self with common sense, 'Is there anything I do, that I know is wrong?' If the answer is yes, it is time to do better and began to learn what holiness is and how it could benefit your lifestyle.

Let Not My Heart Be Trouble

There have been many times in my life when I felt like I did not know which way to go. Day after day there were something happening to me. It seemed like no one could be trusted and I did not know who I could confine in. I had to learn there were decisions to be made; I was not only living for self; but for my family. I wanted my children to be all they could when growing up. I came to realize some things, I could not teach them or how to have that everlasting strength; but to show them who to depend on, and that there will always be a present help. I know that each of them, have their own personalities and that each of us will be walking in different lifestyles but knowing that we still have the same present help gives me hope. Life challenges can knock you down and keep you down if you do not choose to make wiser decisions. I am the type of person that is content if my family is happy. I want to be the one to show my children a better life. During a season in my life, I was full of hurt and anger dealing with people who only tolerated me if it was convenient for them. During this season, I was finding myself arguing and trying to explain myself to others because all I wanted was peace. I began to do things in front of my children that I thought I would never. As a parent I wanted to teach them to stay away from trouble, to stay positive and know themselves and not worrying about people picking at them. At times running into certain people, allowed me to do the very opposite of what I was teaching them. It is alright to stand up for myself, but how I stood made the difference. I began to act just like the very people that was hurting me. I allowed choices I made to develop bad characteristics, that did not define who I truly am. I learned you must be careful who you entertain. During my life trails, being a parent, I knew that there was more to just providing them a place to stay or keeping them well groom and looking decent. I knew making sure they had food to eat was not only what I needed to give them. In this season of my life, I was already attending church but only on special holidays or occasions. I knew just for me alone to overcome this hurt and anger, that I needed to change from within. I knew that I am a good person, I knew how to ignore the evil rumors or the picking, but what I needed help with the most was beyond my control. I was in a position knowing that I could not do it on my own. For me to show my children a better way, I first had to be a partaker in being the example. I started attending Bible Study and Sunday School, along with regular church service. The more I went, the more my mind began to wonder what more I could learn if I started opening up the Holy Bible at home. I felt good, when leaving church. I would go some days feeling sad, but each time during prayer no matter how many times they offered the congregation, I stood in that line wanting others to touch and agree with me. To pray with and for me without judgement.

I decided to start reading the Word of God on my own at home. I would reach a chapter in the morning and before I go to bed. Each time, I would pray through Jesus name for God to give me a clearer understanding of his word. That even if I did not understand it at the time of reading that one day it would make sense to me. I had to have a willing heart to learn. At the moment peace began to enter into my heart, the enemy tried to plot against me. My obstacles still did not stop me from pressing my way in reading God's word. During a particular time in my life I had to attend a class to help me get some type of self-control. I remember it was a Friday and I knew I had to be to another county the next morning for this angry management class; so I took my children to my mother to spend the night, I did not want to awake them early in the morning. When I got back home on that Friday, I began to study the Bible. I can remember it just like yesterday, I read John Chapter 13 prayed over the word for understanding and prepared for bed. While I was asleep,

I received a phone call from a particular person to come to check on other people. After listening to the reason why, the word of God became blank to me. Oh, how easily the enemy had done shift my mind from doing good in trying to change to looking at the bad part about this situation from the phone call. That very same person that I was hanging with and seem not to have liked the same person of interest was with them that night. My mind was so focused on that part of the phone call, that I forgot all about the concern for others and the real reason the person called me. I wanted to confront all parties at the same time to tell them they all belong together, that they were two faced and they needed to hang together. I was missing the picture that the other two individuals had maybe apologized to each other and decided to mend things up. I was focusing on my feelings at this hour and how I felt betrayed. Well as time passed in the midnight hour, I jumped up and got dress ready to confront them, even without their knowledge of this phone call or why I was on my way. I pulled out of my yard and down the road I headed. When I got to the stop signed, my car began to jerk so I turned around and went back home. Because my heart was full of anger, I got in the car again, headed back down the road and again the car started jerking even worse than before. Let me add, at the stop sign there were no streetlights, and could not see anything without my car headlights. I sat there for a moment and turned around at the trash cans that were on the opposite side of the same road. I went back home and was trying to forget about it. I was crying, huffing, and puffing with madness and then the phone rings again. I could have just ignored it but because I am in an outrage, I wanted to hear what they had to say, by this being the same person. Well, they ask me what I am going to do, if I am going to check on these certain people or what. I told them about my car but told them let me try one more time. Little did they know, I was not even really thinking about getting to that location, I wanted to still confront other people. The third time, again at the same place down the road from my residence at the stop sign the car jerking, but this time is shuts off. Now while hurt and anger is lingering in my heart fear jumps in and in that moment my mind began to shift again to seeking help from the Lord above. I began to pray to God, asking him if he could just let this car operate when I crank it, that I would go home and let it go. So, when I tried immediately the car cranked up and I headed back home. That is when I decided in my heart to handle the situation another way.

I began to cry out to the Lord, casting my cares upon him. All the Bible Studies, Sunday School, church services and me reading the word began to flash back in my mind. Me remembering that I can talk to Christ about anything, the good and the bad. I remembered that I could tell Jesus all about it, that he will listen to me, that I did not have to drive around looking for him but to cry out to him and he will be right there. So, I began to fall on my knees and cry asking him why me, the one being signaled out to be mistreated. As, I was crying I started telling him how angry I was and what I wanted to say when I see who I was frustrated with and after all that, I began to calm down in my heart. After, I felt like I got it off my chest, I just started yelling out Jesus, Jesus and kept calling his name. All of sudden it felt like someone was behind me, it brought a little fear because all I could think was did, I leave the door unlock and someone has sneaked into my place. I had to shake myself, so I started back calling on Jesus. I got in the bed without looking back. So when I laid down, I kept calling on the name of Jesus until I fell asleep, then a voice said 'let not your heart be trouble' and felt like someone was rubbing the back of my head to bring me peace as a parent would do their children. I don't particular remembering when I fell asleep but what I do know, I slept like a baby.

The next morning, I woke up and looked at the time, jumped up because I knew that I was going to be late for anger management class. As, I began to head out the door, I remembered that I did not read the chapter for that morning. I told myself, late is late and they may turn me away from entering the classroom, so let me do something right. I open the Bible to the next chapter on my scripture list and it was John 14, so I began to open up the Bible to this chapter. As, soon as I read the first verse at that moment I fell to my knees and cried Holy. I began to repent and surrender myself to God through his son Jesus name. I began to confess my sins and accepted Jesus as my personal Savior. The bless thing about this hour he was still right there, the praise and worship that took place in that hour was the best feeling that I had in my entire life up to this point. After, I got up off the floor, I had to change shirts from all the crying, wiping my face with all the tears, nose running and I felt a release in the spirit of no more burdens on me and I was so excited. I went to my mother house still filled with excitement. When I entered her house and crying she did not know what was going on. I started shouting, she jumped up startled by my actions. After, I calmed down I told her what happen and she started crying with me, then my kids came out the room asking me why I was crying. I told them it was happy tears and that I found a Savior and they would never have to see their mom acting bad no more because in that moment, I had truly been set free. They were happy because I was happy. My mother had to remind me about class. So, I decided to still go. When I got there the day was getting even better. Class had not started the instructor was running late. I was smiling because while others were complaining about leaving and having to wait, I knew it was Jesus favor in my life to let me make it on time. We started passing around a sign in sheet for proof, some began to leave and others, such as myself stayed to wait some more. The instructor arrived and apologize for being late. During class, I was so happy, I was raising my hand on every question he could ask. During our break, he pulled me to the side and ask how I end up in this class and that I was so happy. I shared my good news, and he understood. He let me leave class because he saw that light so bright all around me. I praise Jesus all the way to my mom, picked up my children and we had a good time the rest of the day. I was so excited to get to church that next day for Sunday School to spread the good news. I made it early and told my First Lady about it and I began to tell others and they rejoiced with me before the teaching started. This is how, I surrendered to Christ in my home, from within my heart.

    I want to let you know; He is always here even when we do not look for him. But as soon as we want true help, he will give it to us. I now know the presence of what was behind me that night, it was the presence of Jesus Christ. The word of God confirmed the voice I heard and who was comforting me. I am just so glad, that I went from being angry and doing something wrong, to going into prayer with the one who know all things. It is us who needs to call on him. If you are battling with something and your mind is blank, no matter how hard you think, still feeling empty and just don't know what to do; let me remind you that there is a present help in your presence right now. We got to call on his holy name and tell him all about it. There is nothing too hard for the one who came from heaven to earth to lay down his life for you and me. If you are a nonbeliever, Christ is knocking on your heart to accept him as your personal Savior. To trust in him to fight your battles. He wants you to know you can come to him broken because he loves you. You may be caught up in sin, he still wants you. He wants you as you are, so that he can restore and mold you to whom you should be. Life may put you in a place where it's hard to see your way out, but it is not your place to figure it out, it is your place to seek the answers and apply it to your decisions and the father which is in Heaven will do the rest. He want you to believe in a higher power, believing that he sent his son Jesus to die on the cross for you and that he arose on the third day with all power in his hands, that he ascended to heaven to one day return for you. He is coming back for the true and righteous children. If you are a believer and feel like the weight of the world his upon you, just remember if he brought you through one test, he would surely deliver you from them all. We got to continue believing that these issues are not our battles, but to prepare being equipped the right way to fight. That is why it is important to develop a relationship with him for self. Going to church, studying with others, praying with others and fellowship is part of the encouragement we need from each other; but having that one on one encounter with Christ is far more greater than what any mankind can do for you. You will never want to go back to being your old self. I'm not saying the same situations will go away, but how you respond is not going to be the same. There is nothing too hard for God, just know that you will never take another step alone. He has always been right here with me and you. He doesn't dwell in sin or unrighteousness, but as we call on him for his help, he will direct us in the right path; he will give us the strength to endure all things. He will give us a heart to forgive others as he forgiven us for our sins. Just know, through it all he is here.

How to Stand With Someone Else

In this lifetime as you continue to live and grow, you will come to realize that you are not the only one upon this land that needs a helping hand. Throughout my life, I truly believed that I been chosen to encourage others. As time pass, I have learned that hope can take you a long way. I have learned how to stand with someone else, while Jesus was still in the presence standing for and with me. The Bible tells us in 1 Corinthians 15:14 'Let all that you do be done in love.' God knows, I have not always thought of it that way. I have felt the need to be there for others, just because I thought I had a solution. But as time passed, I learn to stay in my own lane. It is easier to say, that is not my problem; but when you have the love of God within you, you seemed to find your way thinking about other people trials. One thing for sure, I know that I am not God. Therefore, I stay in prayer with the Lord, so that I can help them without saying my thoughts or opinions, but to direct them back to the true help, Christ Jesus.

In my life, I have had the opportunity to help family members, friends, strangers and even my enemies knowing they don't like me or just have that feeling they are trying me. I do not regret one thing I have ever done for someone because I have learned through my mother and growing on my own, to treat others as you want to be treated. I must continue working on when to draw the line. I want to take a moment to share with you, ways that you can stand with someone else.

Prayer is a direct communication between me and Jesus. I have prayed with people by touching and agreeing with them in their presence and by talking to Jesus on their behalf. Also, I have prayed in the presence of people from within, while they are praying. Jesus is one, who you can tell all about it, without others judging you. You can speak to him aloud, or from your heart. He knows the intent of the heart and is in the presence if you want him to be. I have prayed for others without them knowing, a sincere prayer for Jesus to intervene on their circumstances and intercede for them and fight their battles. It is important not to only think of self when praying to Christ. He came from Heaven to earth for all mankind, no one is exempt from being delivered and set free from the enemy (Satan).

Having a listening hear when someone just wants to vent. People are not always looking for a solution, sometimes they just want to be heard. When you began to talk, allow the individual to come to reality of what is happening in their life. The more they speak on it, the more they began to either accept or deny the truth, but still aware the issue is there. Sometimes, you just got to have the listening hear to give them peace. By letting someone else know what they feel, gives them some type of release from the burdens that are pressing heavy on them. Having a listening ear, has help me to know when someone is happy, troubled, or just need someone to talk to. Every conversation is not only about rough days. I had the opportunity of listening to others rejoicing on their success for their accomplishments or something they were interested in. Just being happy to be alive is enough to listen to someone with joy in their heart, knowing how important their life is.

Giving advice from my personal trials or just helping them come up with solutions for what is happening in their lives is another way I have stood with someone. Common sense could help a person figure out their next move. I even learned that sometimes people need that tangible help. Not just saying I am there for you if you need me, call me anytime. Tangible help is giving them a ride because they have no transportation, buying them something to eat because they are hungry. Sometimes people need a financial blessing without paying it back in return because they know where the money needs to go for their household, without being managed or watching every step they make. We are accountable for what we do. Standing in the gap for others requires love and being empathetic with them, not feeling sorry for judging them.

We all have something we need to work on, so there are no way you can say to a person, that they should be able to fight against their struggle, or should have been over it by now. As, stated early I been struggling with my weight for a long time. It has not been a year that has not went by as far as I can think back that I went by without trying to do or try something in losing weight. I have always said I do not believe anyone came into this world to fail. Somethings they have been exposed too and other things because of curiosity may have led them to do what they done. I am not saying that consequences do not follow you, rather it is hard or easy to overcome; I just have learned to pray more and speak less on others situations. Demonic spirits is real and if you don't have any fight in you, you can end up doing harm to self and others. I have learned that sometimes there is no help you can offer someone, but it is through their own belief, prayer, and taking steps will help them get to victory in their life. Cheer them on from the sideline by encouraging them to press their way. Sometime someone could be doing so good and suddenly the worst come. We are not to cast the first stone but lift them up and speak life in them. Letting them know because they live, there is one greater within and if they keep pushing forward, their best is yet to come.

It is so many ways we can stand with someone else, without gossiping about them. Gossip comes in when you want to let the next person know someone else situation, so they could get joy off their downfall or you not trying to figure out what to do to help; but believing it is your place to tell someone else business. Sticks and stones may break my bones, but words would never hurt for me is an understatement. What you say and how you say it, could either build someone up or tear them down. I am not saying it is wrong to call someone out on their wrongdoing because that is when change come; helping someone realize their fault so they could get help.

Just know that He (Jesus) has always been there for us. Before we were even born he knew we were entering a world of destruction, but he still has protected us to come into the knowledge of truth. Jesus have died for all our sins, rather you accept him or not, but still lives on the inside of us. We can never say it is too late for anybody who is breathing. We have no place to put anyone far as I am concern for life after physical death. I used to hear this cliché, that the leaning tree is not always the first to fall. If you mean no good and still trying to get others to recognize the wrong in others, you start to recognize why your life is not altogether. That individual maybe going through a dry season, it is not that time to gloat from their trials.

We all need someone to stand with us in some point in our life, so let us pay the way forward doing it for someone else. Yes, I know it is a lot of evil acts in this world, continue to pray to God to direct your path of whom to be there for and you don't always have to know them to help them. You can donate to charity, take supplies to the school for some innocent child who needs help, or donate to a local food bank. Let us be a cheerful giver, rather it is giving up our time, doing things unseen without telling it, helping in a way that is tangible or intangible. God has us here to be a witness and being able to stand for someone else gives them that hope to face the moment they are in.

COVID-19, I Was Not Exempt

As soon as I received the phone call and the doctor stated I tested positive, all I could say is huh, what. Suddenly, my mind reflected to me informing my boss that I was ordered to quarantine for 14 days and that I had to be tested. I could remember me telling him, I know that I will be negative. Then human reaction kicked in, tears began to roll down my face. I was shocked and all type of things began to wonder in my mind. I was wondering who I should call first because I had to tell someone. Soon as I got off the phone with my doctor, I received a phone call from Public Health, with so many questions and procedures I had to follow. While they were asking me questions, I was asking them some too because this thing called COVID-19 had overtook my life. I had to inform my job, people that I have been contact with during a certain time period and if I could not reached them, I had to let the Public Health know, so they could and they did.

I can remember me going to the doctor early in the month of March, due to me coughing. During pollen season, I always have cough sneeze, watery eyes, occasional sneezing, and runny nose, so I stay drinking water and washing my face. Although my allergies always bother me during this season, I went and got tested for the flu and the results came back negative. I was given some medicine to help me because I was having this aching feeling in my body, coughing and I could remember my stomach hurting. Because of the wheezing in my chest, I end up getting a home Nebulizer for breathing treatment with other medication to follow. Weeks passed by and still this cough will come and go. It felt normal because this happens every year around this time. I go back to the doctor because I am feeling really tired at work. My chest began hurting due to all the coughing, so I called my boss to get off because I am not feeling normal anymore. My daughter called me that same day, telling me to go to the doctor because the day before, I told her I could not smell when I disinfected the office at work or taste my lunch that was made. She did not want to alarm me but instructed me to make an appointment to visit my local physician. I told her I did, and I was headed there soon. When I got to the doctor, I immediately get a mask upon entering due to other people already there. Others was setting in their vehicles. Once I was in the patient's room, and I began to tell them what's wrong, completing that COVID-19 questionnaire sheet and the doctor listening to my chest. I had to go and get some chest x-rays and got two shots. Later on that evening, I got a phone called explaining that my chest x-ray shows that I got bronchitis. This same day I began the 14 day quarantine and was scheduled to get tested for COVID-19 on the next day. I called my family and informed them. I wished that I would have seen them earlier that week instead of talking to them on the phone because now for the next fourteen days I couldn't have any contact and was ordered to stay home alone. My youngest daughter refused to leave me home alone and so we came up with a plan of how we were going to stay in the same place and not see each other. We would call each other, before we step out our rooms. When we used the bathroom, we would be responsible for disinfecting it, each night we had to wash our own laundry. First, we would cook at different times, then she thought it would be best to bring my food to the door because we did not want me to take the chance of cooking and getting over heated. My son, who lives with me as well, had left to stay with his sister's days prior because the air conditioning unit in our home was not working.

The next day, I got tested, picked up my prescribed medication at the drive thru and went back home. Days continued to pass. I was trying to feel as normal as I could but my chest was still sore due to the coughing and bronchitis. I could feel my body beginning to ache like I had the flu. On Tuesday morning, I called and left message for the doctor to call me. I wanted to see if they could prescribe me another dose of muscle relaxer. I could feel my body getting stiff. When the doctor returned my phone call, I thought they were responding to my phone call but no, that was not the case. This call was to inform me that I was COVID-19 positive. It's amazing how so much can rush through your mind. I was thinking, this cannot be, not me.

How could this be. After speaking with the doctor, immediately I get a phone call from Department of Public Health and if felt like I was being interrogated but I know they was doing their job. I followed all protocol that the doctor told me and notified my job and anyone I had come in contact of my results. I forgot all about addressing the issue about my body aching

On that Wednesday, I literally had to drag myself to the bathroom with no strength, holding on to the wall because I did not want to tell my daughter. When I finally got to the bathroom, only thing I can do is fall on the toilet. My daughter thought I had fell and she jumped up and asked me was I alright. I told her, yeah just tired and sore. She said that she was getting dressed and coming out to make sure I was okay, but I told her no, we had a plan and if I really needed her I will let her know. I was breathing so hard and it seemed as if I could not catch my breath. By the time, I got off that toilet and looked at my urine; I knew what was put me in a heavy breathing mood. I was having shortness of breath already just trying to make it to the bathroom, but my urine was the color of dark soda like Pepsi. I did not know what to do or what to think. At this time, I ease my way to the recliner to get a hold of myself and try to catch my breath. By this time, the Office Manager called to check on me and she could hear me breathing hard and suggested that I go to the hospital and I told her that I did not want to get admitted. So, she put me on the phone with my doctor, she could hear the same thing and then I told her about my urine. I really did not want to go the hospital but I am glad, I did. My doctor, told me to hang up and call the ambulance and she would notify the hospital that I was on my way. By my mind stuck on the pain and my urine, I end up calling the hospital and they had to tell me to dial 911. By this time, my daughter had come out the room suited in personal protective gear. She was covered like the nurses, gloves on, mask on, hair covered, double long sleeve and pants. She called 911 because I was still breathing fast and having shortness of breath. She notified the ambulance that I was COVID-19 positive. A team arrived before my pickup ambulance arrived. They were all suited up and treated me like I was somebody. When, I arrived to the hospital they already had a room and started waiting on me immediately.

During my five nights of staying, so much began to take place in my body. My liver enzymes began to increase, fighting this virus. I did not have strength to walk. My nurses had to change my bed linen while I was on the bed. I was not put on a ventilator, but I had to get oxygen at night. I am so glad that I never caught a fever. I had to get medicine in my IV and by mouth. Waking up, every morning getting blood drawn and getting chest x-rays. My food arrived in plastic to-go plates on plastic trays because what entered the room, was disregarded and it had to stay in the room because the hospital had a protocol to go by. Any way they could prevent the spread was a safety precaution. I did not have time to call everyone. I had to focus on my health, and I began to pray and tell Jesus, "I want to live and not die." Even though, I repent daily but I told him, if anything I done wrong that did not please him, to please forgive me. My focus was on my true help in the time of trouble and I truly believe, Jesus was the source of my strength. I showed the Lord how grateful I was to have the activity of my limbs. I had to keep moving forward. It went from the nurses washing me, to me telling them to let me wash what I could, and they could help me with the rest. It went from washing laying down, to sitting in the chair. I started going to the bathroom more. It went from them helping me to me using a walker to doing it on my own. I wanted to express my gratitude to Christ for his love and mercy towards me. Even, while being in intensive care you have to make a code for your family to call you. I wanted to show Christ, how much I believed, I made my code the word 'healed'. I knew if I talked to some of my friends and family, their love and concern for me would of showed in their voice and if I heard them crying or even sympathizing because of this condition, that would of made me feel the same way. I had to stay strong, it wasn't that I wanted certain people to know, but I knew what were best for me. I was able to draw strength from my children, my mother and husband, because each night they group called me; while, one song a gospel song, the other chose each night who would pray and the rest will read scriptures to me. Sometimes the enemy will still try to distract you, but I give a shot out to my sister Jennifer from another mother, who was led by the spirit to call me not knowing what was going on with me. She began to pray with and for me, strength began to come from everywhere.

While being in the hospital, the spirit of the Lord began to remind me of scriptures and stories in the Bible. By me not having one, I began to take notes in my phone, so I could remember to study the scriptures, whenever I went home. I looked them up and began to read and study. It felt like God wanted me to give my testimony and to inform others what the word was speaking to me and to others on his timing. First, I remember the Scripture, Mark 5: 36 came to mind 'Do not be afraid just believe'. I say this statement all the time because I have it hanging on my wall. As, I began to read the scripture, I started at the twenty-first verse all the way through the forty-third verse. There was a ruler by the name of Jairus, whom had this daughter who was at a point of facing death in her life. He fell at Jesus feet. Jesus began to go with him, and while going to meet the need of this ruler; here comes a certain woman who touched him. This woman was facing an issue for twelve long years wanted to just touch the hem of his garment. She did not even think about interrupting him on his journey. All she need was to touch him, to be connected to him. Jesus asked, 'who touched my clothes?' Already knowing who it was, she too fell before him and told the truth. Jesus wants us to continue casting our cares to him, he wants us to bow down to him and repent, confess our sins to him. This woman came one way, being a certain woman, but Jesus said, 'Daughter that her faith has made her whole, go in peace and be whole of thy plague.' Jesus went back tending to the ruler, by the time he got there she was already dead. The people began to ask him, why trouble the master. Little did they know, He is the master. Jesus put them all out and took the father and mother in and told the daughter to arise. After she did, he told her to go feed her. I believe what God is trying to tell us that in order to grow we got to let doubt and fear cease. Even down to other people, doubting what he can do. We need people to build us up. As, I continue to read, I noticed that the daughter was of the age twelve. Now, I started my quarantine on the twenty-fifth of March, got put in the hospital and released on the sixth day of April, in which twelve days had passed. I began to know in my spirit, God is going to do a new thing in me. Its more that I got to do than live in the norm. I will not go back being the same. He wants me to bring hope, in what seems to be hopeless situation. It is time for me to speak life and encourage others to a better future.

The second story, I was reminded of when Jesus heals the man who was born blind. You can find that story in the book of John, one of the four gospels. I read John, chapter nine, verse one through twelve. The verse that stood out to me, was verse three after the disciples began to question Jesus on who sinned for this to happen to this man. Jesus replied, 'neither hath this man sinned, nor his parents: but the works of God should be made manifest in him.' Sickness doesn't always come because of sin. God can use a situation and show his mercy, love, and his power. Sometimes, the good and righteous suffer with the bad. God must show up and demonstrate that he is our help and that we can trust him in all things. COVID-19 is growing rapidly around this world. No one asked for this, God does not have a respected person. This sickness can attack anybody. No one is exempt, that is why it is very important to trust God at all times. I did nothing wrong to deserve this, so I had to focus on getting better instead of the pain that I was going through in this moment of my life.

The third story I read, was about the parable of the ten virgins. You can find this story in Matthew, chapter twenty-five, verses one through thirteen. All the ten virgins knew the bridegroom was coming. That is just like we all are aware of this virus going around. We all are receiving the same information and instructions to follow. We are all notified to wash our hands often, to stay social distancing at least six feet apart, to stay at home, unless it is necessary to get essentials or to meet our medical needs. Anything that will help prevent the spread, even down to wearing mask. We knew nothing about this thing called COVID-19 was going to creep into this world. That is why we got to be ready. Among these virgins, were five wise and ready waiting on the bridegroom, stored up with their oil. The oil was their faith and belief that Christ was going to appear. Then, there was five foolish that was not ready. They wanted to get oil from the wise, but the wise knew what they needed in order to see the bridegroom. So the foolish, had to scatter themselves to find some oil, which caused them to be locked out by the time they returned. See, we got to get connected to Jesus for ourselves. Holiness is right and a way of living. That is why scripture tells us, choose this day whom you will serve. When afflictions come upon us, we must be ready to trust in the Lord and be in a position for him to respond to our call.

In other words, we got to learn to focus on the good. I was praising Jesus for being alive. He wants us not to take for granted the things we cannot touch but could do with action. He wants us to study his word more, so that we can develop a deeper relationship with him. He wants us to love without judgement. Love covers a multitude of sin. He wants us to forgive, so that our heart will not be harden. The same as he forgiven us for our sins, he wants us to do the same to others. He wants us to have quality time with the people in our home, getting to know them better. He wants us to communicate more with him in prayer and to our loves one. It is time to stop having quick and microwave conversations and get to know him and each other better. He wants us to self-discipline ourselves. We are always moving at a fast pace. It is time to slow down and enjoy life. You do not have to buy or go somewhere to be happy. He wants us to seek that inner joy and peace with him. Being home should be a blessing to us, being around the one is we love, learning how to be patient with one another because of different personalities and choices in life.

After arriving home from the hospital, my body still has not recovered all my strength. But God, still had a way in me making progress. My caseworker and doctors knew I needed help at home. Arrangements for a nurse and physical therapist was made for me. They would come to my home and work with me on building my strength and balance back. I truly am so thankful for Optim Health, Dr. Sherma Peters and staff, East Georgia Regional Medical Center, Statesboro Ambulance services, the EMT responding and Suncrest Home Health for being here for me in a time of need. I went from being weak to now strong. I too am thankful for my family, the prayer warriors from my church, True Love Tabernacle Deliverance Center, my job, friends and other people that knew about my circumstances as they began to speak life in me and gave me encouragement with great hope that everything was going to be alright. To

God be the glory that I am healed from this sickness and that I can tell others to keep hope in their hearts.

Lukewarm Just Won't Do

For God so loved the world that he gave his only son, so that we may live and not die. We all have a purpose on this earth, we were born for greatness. During my lifetime, I have faced many trails and did not know how to handle some of them. It was strange that I would have faith in some situations and others seem like, I could not survive. Accepting Christ as my personal Savior required me to fully accept and understand that my life was not my own. I had to allow the Holy Spirit to lead me in spirit and truth through developing a relationship with Christ and allow the Holy Bible to be my guide. It did not work the way I thought it would because I truly did not understand the fullness and power of God. I did not fully understand the saying, come as you are and surrender all. It would be at times in my life, that I was living what seemed as a good and decent life such as : staying out of trouble, being kind and nice to others and keeping peace between me and all I came in contact with in the presence or communicating through other ways, such as phone, letter or social media. I come to realize that was not enough. It is so important to hide the word of God in your heart. It is a reminder of what God expects of me. When, I first truly accepted Christ in my life, I was so excited and glad the sudden change and strength that I had. Little, did I know that it would not be easy every day, in making the right decision that would please God and having an ear when the spirit was speaking to me. I could remember compromising my promises to God, to make me feel comfortable around others or trying to make them feel easy being around me by accepting the change that I made in my life. The Bible let us know that we can love without judging, we can show love to all mankind without decreasing your walk with God. I had the feeling of not making anyone feel like they don't want to be around me because of my change. I can remember how quickly, I would get caught up in doing worldly things in the presence of others; not because they made me react that way, but just wanted to be accepted. In those moments I realize I was not living a Holy life or stronger in Christ than I thought. I can remember attending different functions and certain music would come on and straightway my mind would go back down memory lane. The more I thought back, the more the flesh came subject to the world, then I find myself back doing the same thing, on the dance floor dropping like its hot, as people called it, or engaging in conversation about my past and laughing about all the wrong I done, as if I did not have a care in the world. It was like suddenly I forgot that I repented for those things. It was not that I was better than anyone, but it was me who chose to surrender my life, so that Christ would lead me. Those moments made me realize that it was more than just being a model citizen and doing good deeds. I had to make a choice daily, to allow God to rule and abide in me.

In the book of Revelation, Jesus talks to seven different churches, applauding them for their good but also warning them, what they needed help in; so they can grow from their weakness, to repent and move forward in growing more spiritually in him. As Jesus was ministering to The Church of Laodicea, he let them know how pleased he was of them being true and faithful witnesses. Because they were a wealthy city, they felt the need of wanting for nothing. This allowed them to get far away from the spiritual truth. Their inner man was becoming weaker because of living in the natural and thinking all their needs was being met. Jesus wanted them to repent and move toward depending on him. He began to describe their life being neither cold nor hot. He compared it to being lukewarm, meaning they did not know which way they wanted to live. He would rather for us to be cold or hot for him, not in between. In the scriptures, it lets us know to either accept or deny him, we cannot just tag along to whatever benefits us. If you want to sit on His throne, life after death from this physical body, we must make a choice how to live. I had to pray to God that I would show love and fellowship with my family and friends and not compromise the life that I had chosen. I would accept Christ and seek his will daily for my life. I had to pray for self-discipline and how to rebuke the flesh from overpowering the spirit. Flesh and spirit, wrestle against each other daily. That is why it important to pray, fast and repent. When the Holy Spirit, stand up within us, it gives us warning of when we are going down the wrong path. It gives us the opportunity to turn from the wicked ways and seek the path of righteous. The enemy job is to distract us from experiencing what God has for us. He attempts to sneak in, to make you get caught messing up and feel bad about self, like it is no way out. We cannot allow any demonic spirit to overpower our lives, but to let the power of the blood of Jesus and the Holy Spirit lift a standard within us to overcome evil with good. We must trust in Christ to intercede on our behalf to help us make the right decision. Jesus want the Laodicea to repent and to be restored through their faith and fellowship with Christ to lead them on.

I can attest that Jesus is still here in my presence, to help me through everything. I have learned how to talk to him daily, casting my cares to him, to praising him for his goodness, his mercy, grace, and forgiveness of my sins. I rejoice, just knowing that I have someone, I can talk to without being judged. If we continue to accept him to be the head of our lives, He will be with us until the end.

It's A War Going On

Everybody is at war or has been at war with his or her flesh sometime during their lives, rather it's from daily living or having to make a personal decision and reflecting on the outcome. My heart goes out to everyone because we all have our own perspective on situations, ideas or actions that must be taken. How we fight and what we stand for will be the focus point on this war.

The first battle, I want to talk about is the war you can't see; but it has a really big effect of how we respond, this is called the battle of the mind. What you ponder on and think can allow belief, hurt, anger or misconception and many other actions. It can also lead to other territories you never would've imagine. People are angry and hurt about things that has happened to them or others they care about, until their thoughts and eyes have been clouded with animosity.

Another battle that we can physically see is, prejudice, hate, power of authority and inequality. I recently communicated with my children and informed them to to seek God for strength to stand for what is right. I remember going over the parable about David and Goliath, when David had to fight this big giant Goliath. Saul and his army seem to be facing fear against the Philistines. So, when David had the courage to step up, they thought he was not ready but he had to remind them what happen to him, while doing his other job. David defeated Goliath and brought his head to show that he won the battle. In other words, I wanted to teach them some things you got to face in life and that God will be there when you need him. With all the killings going on, all the prejudice and racial slurs being said with no remorse; shows the true intent of that person's heart. While all these innocent lives being taken, media and the ones who doing wrong coming up with excuses; a man with a not so good past to what media says, still spark the nation. It is very important to have a voice and knowing the difference between protesting and rioting. I truly understand people react in different ways and it is their prerogative. I wanted them to be aware of the injustice that is happening across this nation and how we could help so we attended a peaceful protest in our hometown. It is important to understand that God created us all and we were all wonderfully made. No one is the same, when one hurt we all should hurt. It is okay to be angry, scream and do other things, as long as the reaction makes a positive difference. We are to never react to what we disagree in a negative way. If we could show love to the very thing we object, the wrongful act, to those who are doing it; by standing against it, we can all make a change and impact. We all have a voice, so by speaking up could bring awareness to the situation.

We are at war spiritually. I don't go against anyone for what or who they believe in, I am here to speak on who and what has kept me. If it had not been for Jesus, I would have been lost my mind a long time ago. In order to win this spiritual battle, you got to be equipped and ready for war. In my life I have dealt with so many things. I want to make it clear, I have far more better days than bad days and each day I live is a blessing. With so much happening on this earth, we are going to need that supernatural strength to keep us standing strong looking forward to our eternal life and not this life only on earth. As you can see by reading, some of the many trials and strongholds was defeated due to my belief in Jesus, the one who intercedes and fights our battles. I see people who inspired others to live right, falling for anything or have turned their back on God because of light afflictions or because things did not go their way. To fight these wars, we cannot think on our own, we got to seek counsel from above, so it could direct us and set us apart from how the world will handle it. Even Jesus won the war by consulting with the Father, before making a decision. Some battles cause a quick response, while others need to wait for directions. We got to understand that we are stronger than any war, we face. As, we keep on living we will learn what battles to respond to and what does not deserve a response at all. We got to get right and ready. If we are not developing strong standards and morals, to help examine ourselves, we will end up losing in the end. Let us not get caught up in the moment, to lose focus on what is best and the effect it has on others. Everybody goes through something, but how we fight is what matters.

To The Reader

I send greetings and my love to you for supporting me, by reading and taking a sneak peak into my life and how Jesus has been there through it all. I will never have enough words to tell you all, what he has done for me. I can tell you, I am so grateful he saved a wretch like me and took my sins to the cross; that he rose on the third day with all power in his hand, that I too have the opportunity to be with him one day.

To the believers of Christ, let us continue to run this race with patience. To be a light to a dark world. To pray to God, to allow you to build up others and introduce them to him. We must live in a way that pleases him. Let us not get so comfortable that we feel like we have arrived, and we are just waiting. Every day is a new day to live in righteousness. Let us stay focus, remembering Jesus is still here through it all.

Note To Self

JESUS IS THERE THROUGH IT ALL

www.ingramcontent.com/pod-product-compliance
Lightning Source LLC
Chambersburg PA
CBHW072019290426
44109CB00018B/2289